ESTATE   PUBLICATIONS

SHREWSBURY

BOMERE HEATH · SHAWBURY

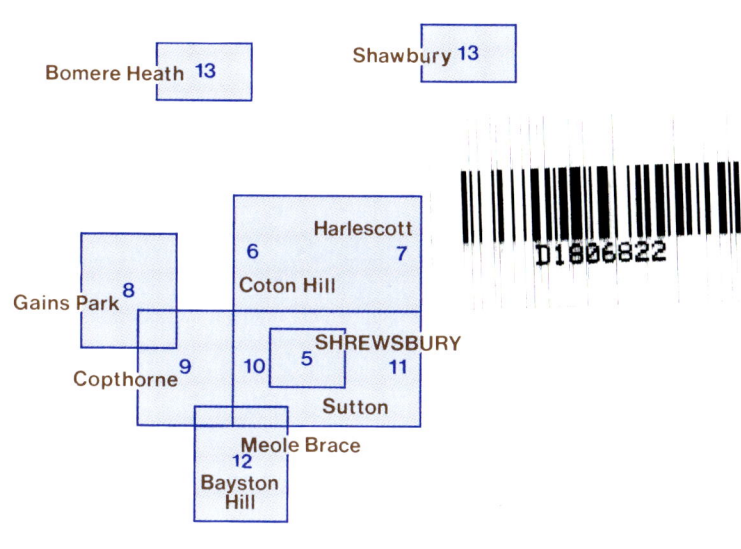

Bomere Heath 13

Shawbury 13

Harlescott

6   7

Coton Hill

Gains Park 8

SHREWSBURY

Copthorne 9   10   5   11

Sutton

Meole Brace
12
Bayston
Hill

ROAD MAP	page 2 – 3
SHREWSBURY ENLARGED CENTRE	page 5
STREET INDEX	page 14–15

One-way street	→
Post Office	●
Church	✚
Pedestrian Precinct	▨
Public Convenience	Ⓒ
Car Park	Ⓟ
Scale of Street Maps: 4 inches to 1 Mile	

Street plans prepared and published by ESTATE PUBLICATIONS, Bridewell House, Tenterden, Kent and based upon the ORDNANCE SURVEY maps with the sanction of the controller of H.M. Stationery Office.

The publishers acknowledge the co-operation of Shrewsbury & Atcham Borough Council in the preparation of these maps.

0 86084 373 4

Babbinswood
Kenwick
English Frankton
Cockshutt
Loppington
5 B5065
Wem
Aston
Weston
682
Rednal
Lower Hordley
Noneley
Lee Brockhurst
Haughton
Bagley
Petton
Burlton
Booley
Preston Brockhurst
MONTGOMERYSHIRE CANAL "under restoration"
West Felton
Weston Lullingfields
Alderton
Clive
Moreton Corbet
Stanton Hine
Eardiston
Wykey
Myddle
Yorton
Grinshill
Shawbury
Edg
Knockin
Stanwardine in the Fields
450
Baschurch
Harmer Hill
Merrington
13
Mucklet
Kinnerley
Ruyton-XI-Towns
8 Prescott
Walford
Preston Gubbals
Hadnall
Astley
Gre Wyth
Crosslanes
Little Ness
Bomere Heath
10
Poynton Green
Hig Erc
Nesscliffe
Great Ness
Yeaton
Leaton
Albrighton
8
Haughton
Roden
Pentre
Felton Butler
12
Ensdon
Fitz
Battlefield
Rodington
Melverley
Shrawardine
Forton
Bicton
Uffington
Crew Green
Alberbury
Montford
Ford
SHROPS
Wit
Wollaston
Cardeston
Ford
10
SHREWSBURY
Upton Magna
Walc
Halfway House
Nox
Cruckton
Meole Brace
A5
Norton
Vennington
Stretton Heath
Yockleton
Cruckmeole
Hanwood
Bayston Hill
Atcham
Upp
Westbury
Stoney Stretton
Edge
Lea
9
Annscroft
Wroxeter
Cross Houses
Donni
5
Farley
Hinton
Plealey
Great Lyth
559
Berrington
Condover
12
Ea Consta
Aston Rogers
Westley
Asterley
Pontesbury
Longden
Cound
Brook
Cantlop
18
Minsterley
A488
1049
Oaks
Stapleton
Pitchford
Golding
Cressat
Worthen
Ploxgreen
Habberley
514
Dorrington
Acton Burnell
Acton Pigott
Cound
9
Leigh
Hope
Pulverbatch
Church Pulverbatch
13
Longnor
Frodesley
Ruckley
Kenley
Ha
Snailbeach
Meadowtown
12
Gravels
Pennerley
1647
Picklescott
Woolstaston
Leebotwood
Church Preen
Hughley
Stret Westw
Black Marsh
Shelve
1762
Ratlinghope
1236
Enchmarsh
Plaish
The Bog
Bridges
1506
Cardington
Gretton
13
Easthop
Linley Hill
1349
1694
Church Stretton
All Stretton
Longville in the Dale
Linley
Norbury
Hope Bowdler
Wall Bank
17
W

©Estate Publications

ESTATE PUBLICATIONS

STREET ATLASES

ASHFORD, TENTERDEN
BASILDON, BRENTWOOD
BASINGSTOKE, ANDOVER
BOURNEMOUTH, POOLE, CHRISTCHURCH
BRIGHTON, LEWES, NEWHAVEN, SEAFORD
BROMLEY (London Borough),
CHELMSFORD, BRAINTREE, MALDON, WITHAM
CHICHESTER, BOGNOR REGIS
COLCHESTER, CLACTON
CRAWLEY & MID SUSSEX
DERBY, HEANOR, CASTLE DONNINGTON
EDINBURGH
EXETER, EXMOUTH
FAREHAM, GOSPORT
FOLKESTONE, DOVER, DEAL
GLOUCESTER, CHELTENHAM
GRAVESEND, DARTFORD
GUILDFORD, WOKING
HASTINGS, EASTBOURNE, HAILSHAM
HIGH WYCOMBE
I. OF WIGHT TOWNS
LEICESTER
MAIDSTONE
MANSFIELD
MEDWAY, GILLINGHAM
NEW FOREST
NOTTINGHAM, EASTWOOD, HUCKNALL, ILKESTON
OXFORD
PLYMOUTH, IVYBRIDGE, SALTASH, TORPOINT
PORTSMOUTH, HAVANT
READING
REIGATE, BANSTEAD, REDHILL
RYE & ROMNEY MARSH
ST. ALBANS, WELWYN, HATFIELD
SALISBURY, AMESBURY, WILTON
SEVENOAKS
SHREWSBURY
SLOUGH, MAIDENHEAD
SOUTHAMPTON, EASTLEIGH
SOUTHEND-ON-SEA
SWALE (Sittingbourne, Faversham, I. of Sheppey)
SWINDON
TELFORD
THANET, CANTERBURY, HERNE BAY, WHITSTABLE
TORBAY
TUNBRIDGE WELLS, TONBRIDGE, CROWBOROUGH
WATFORD, HEMEL HEMPSTEAD
WINCHESTER, NEW ALRESFORD
WORTHING, LITTLEHAMPTON, ARUNDEL

COUNTY ATLASES

AVON
AVON & SOMERSET
BERKSHIRE
CHESHIRE
CORNWALL
DEVON
DORSET
ESSEX
HAMPSHIRE
HERTFORDSHIRE
KENT (64pp)
KENT (128pp)
OXFORDSHIRE
SHROPSHIRE
SOMERSET
SURREY
SUSSEX (64pp)
SUSSEX (128pp)
WILTSHIRE

LEISURE MAPS

SOUTH EAST (1:200,000)
KENT & EAST SUSSEX (1:150,000)
SURREY & SUSSEX (1:150,000)
SOUTHERN ENGLAND (1:200,000)
ISLE OF WIGHT (1:50,000)
WESSEX (1:200,000)
DEVON & CORNWALL (1:200,000)
CORNWALL (1:180,000)
DEVON (1:200,000)
DARTMOOR & SOUTH DEVON COAST (1:100,000)
GREATER LONDON (1:80,000)
EAST ANGLIA (1:250,000)
THAMES & CHILTERNS (1:200,000)
COTSWOLDS & WYEDEAN (1:200,000)
HEART OF ENGLAND (1:250,000)
WALES (1:250,000)
THE SHIRES OF MIDDLE ENGLAND (1:250,000)
SHROPSHIRE, STAFFORDSHIRE (1:200,000)
SNOWDONIA (1:125,000)
YORKSHIRE & HUMBERSIDE (1:250,000)
YORKSHIRE DALES (1:125,000)
NORTH YORK MOORS (1:125,000)
NORTH WEST ENGLAND (1:200,000)
ISLE OF MAN (1:60,000)
NORTH PENNINES & LAKES (1:200,000)
LAKE DISTRICT (1:75,000)
BORDERS OF ENGLAND & SCOTLAND (1:200,000)
BURNS COUNTRY (1:200,000)
ISLE OF ARRAN (1:63,360)
ARGYLL & THE ISLES (1:200,000)
HEART OF SCOTLAND (1:200,000)
GREATER GLASGOW (1:150,000)
LOCH LOMOND & TROSSACHS (1:150,000)
PERTHSHIRE (1:150,000)
FORT WILLIAM, BEN NEVIS, GLEN COE (1:185,000)
IONA (1:10,000) & MULL (1:115,000)
GRAMPIAN HIGHLANDS (1:185,000)
LOCH NESS & INVERNESS (1:150,000)
AVIEMORE & SPEY VALLEY (1:150,000)
SKYE & LOCHALSH (1:130,000)
CAITHNESS & SUTHERLAND (1:185,000)
WESTERN ISLES (1:125,000)
ORKNEY & SHETLAND (1:128,000)
ENGLAND & WALES (1:650,000)
SCOTLAND (1:500,000)
GREAT BRITAIN (1:1,100,000)

ROAD ATLAS

MOTORING IN THE SOUTH (1:200,000)

EUROPEAN LEISURE MAPS

EUROPE (1:3,100,000)
BENELUX (1:600,000)
FRANCE (1:1,000,000)
GERMANY (1:1,000,000)
GREECE & THE AEGEAN (1:1,000,000)
IRELAND (1:625,000)
ITALY (1:1,000,000)
MEDITERRANEAN CRUISING (1:5,000,000)
SCANDINAVEA (1:2,600,000)
SPAIN & PORTUGAL (1:1,000,000)
THE ALPS (1:1,000,000)
THE WORLD (1:35,000,000)
THE WORLD FLAT SHEET

ESTATE PUBLICATIONS are also
sole distributors in the U.K. for:
ORDNANCE SURVEY, Republic of Ireland
ORDNANCE SURVEY, Northern Ireland

Catalogue and prices from ESTATE PUBLICATIONS,
Bridewell House, Tenterden, Kent TN30 6JB.
Tel: 05806 4225   Fax: 05806 3720

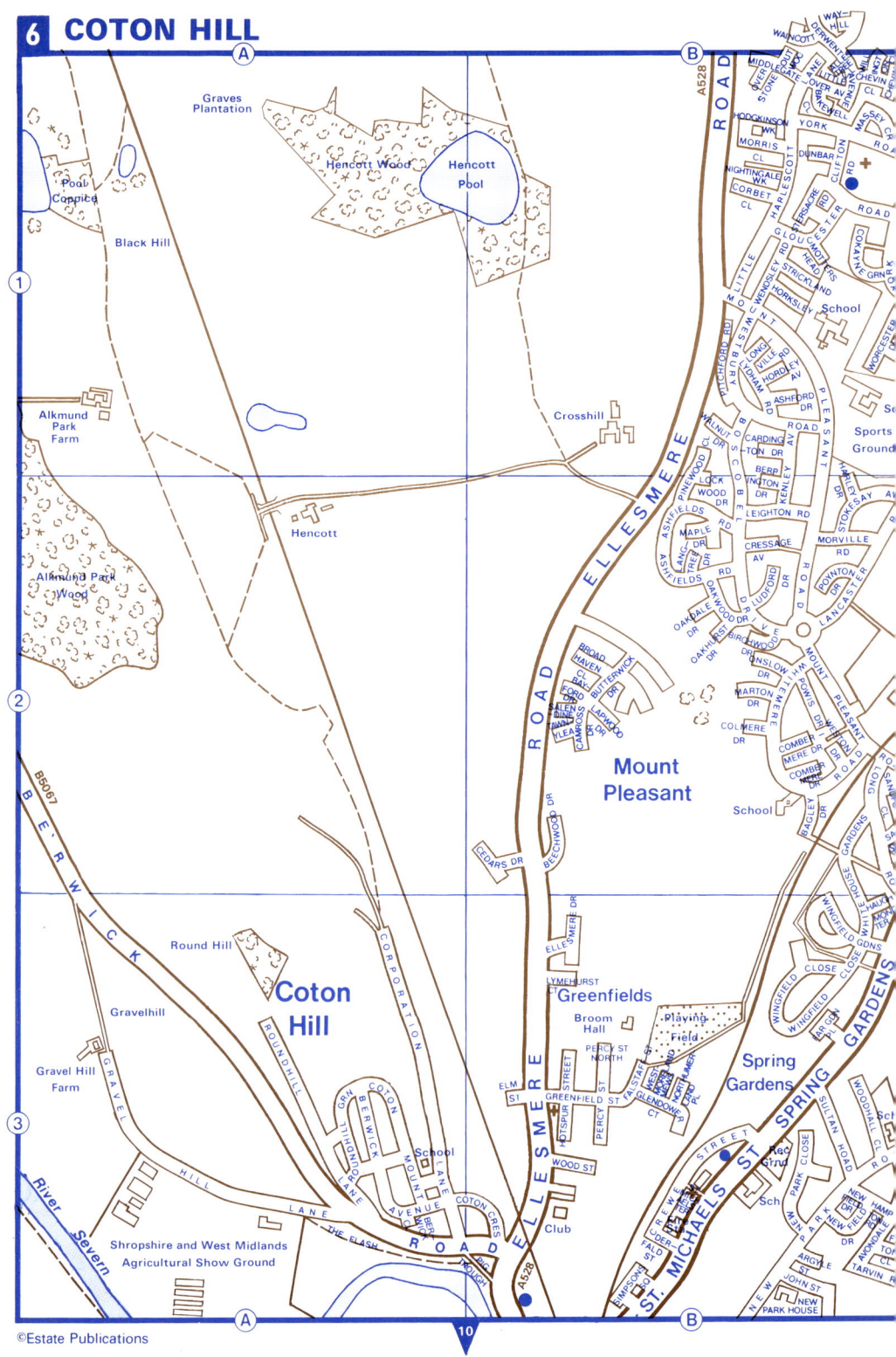

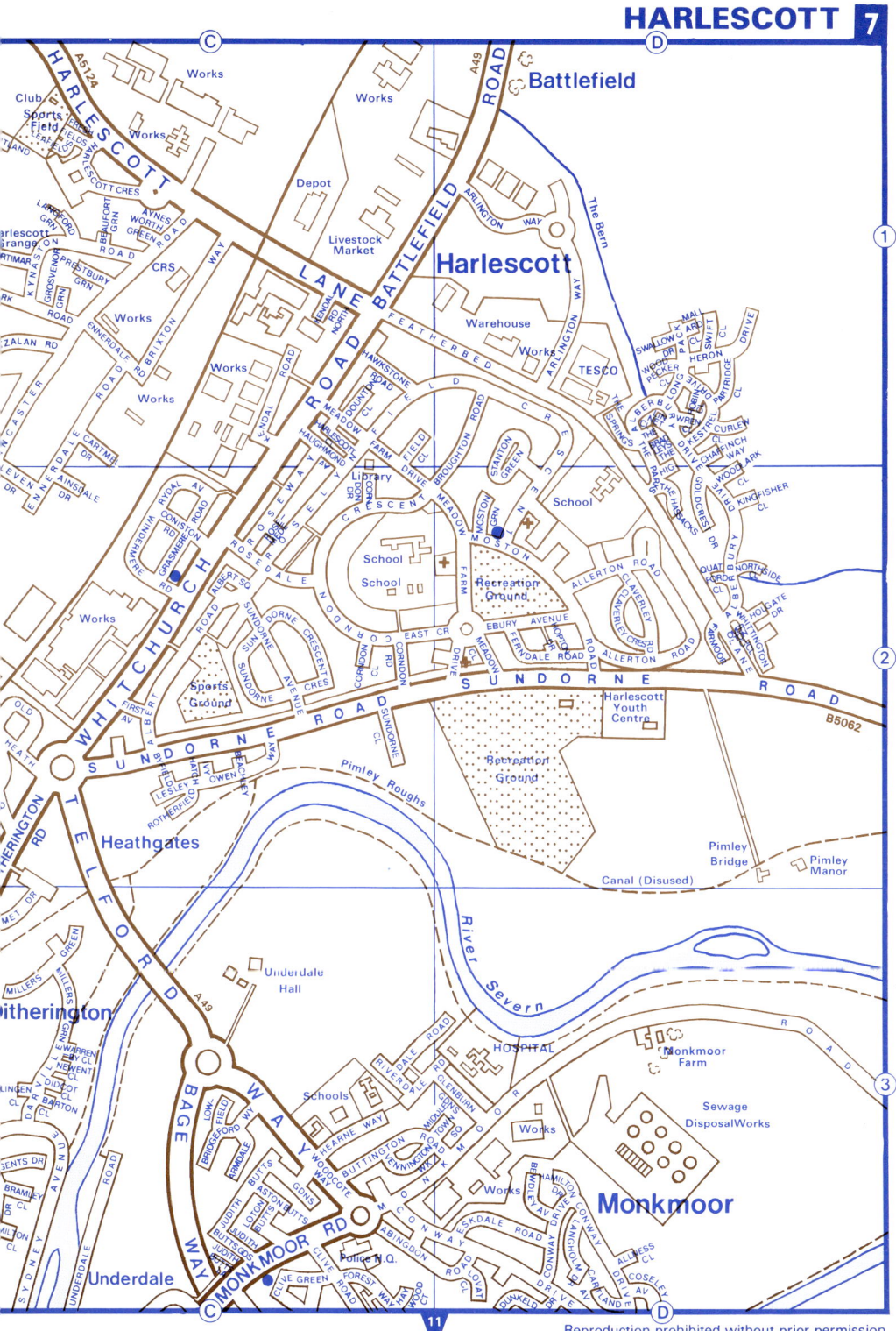

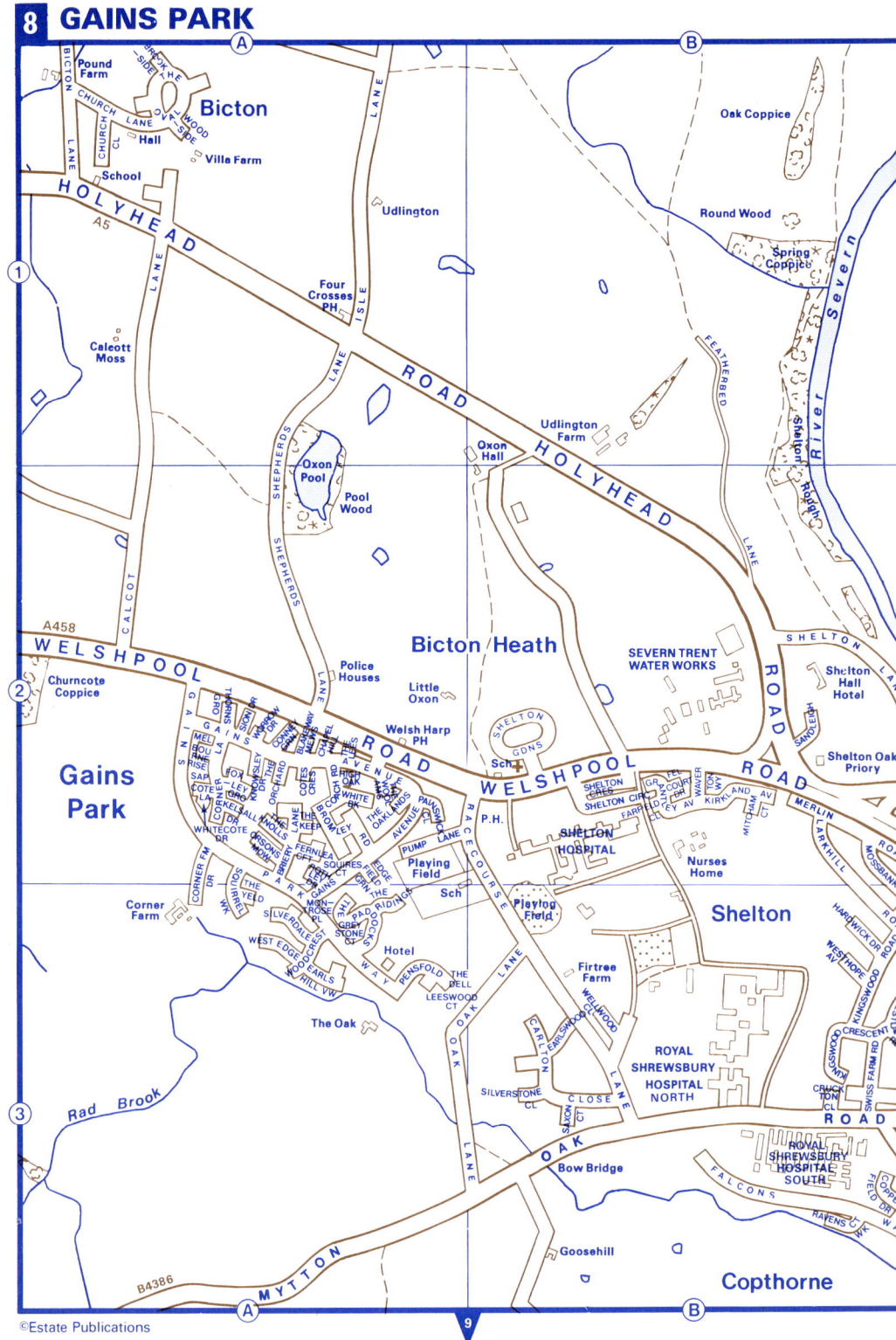

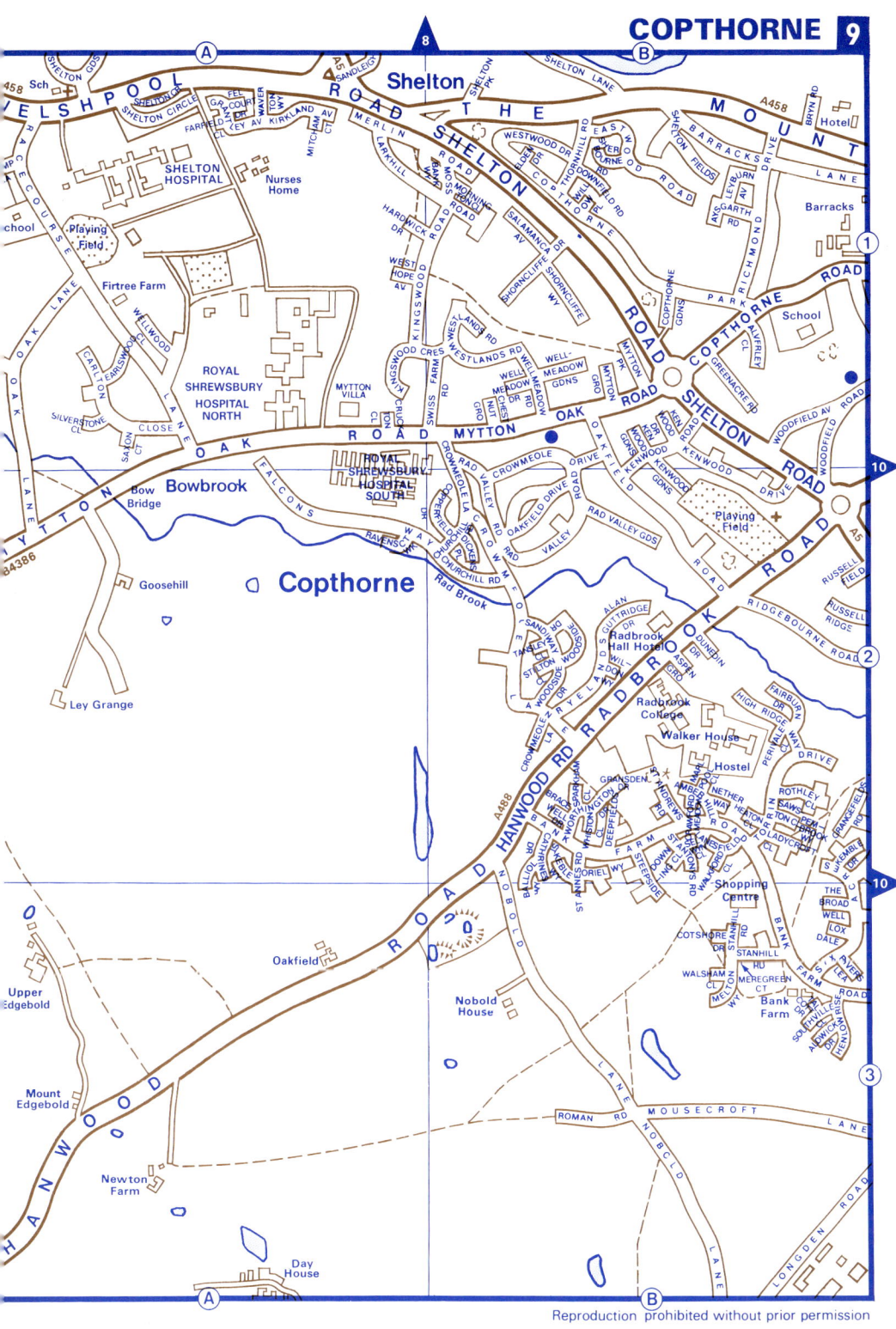

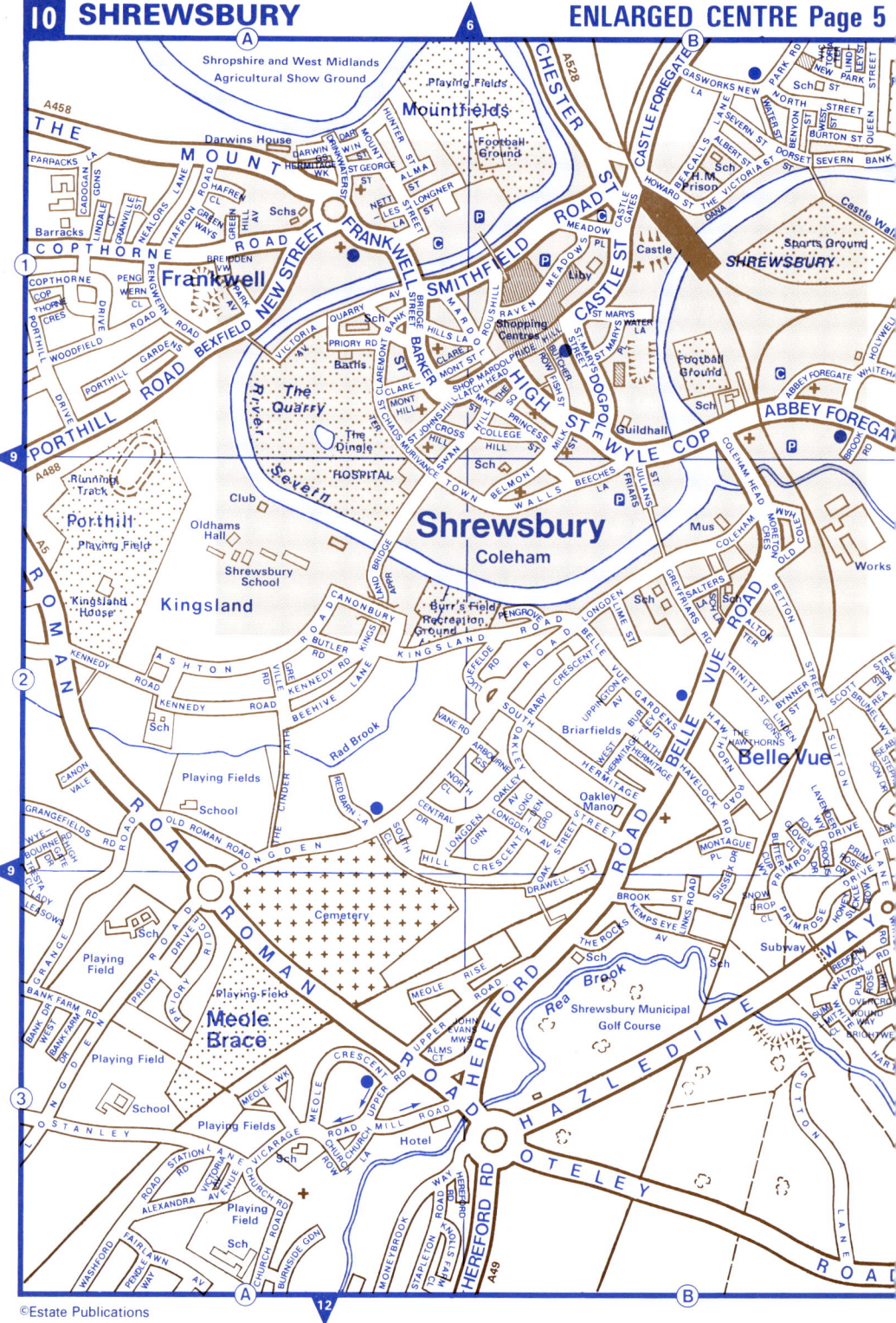

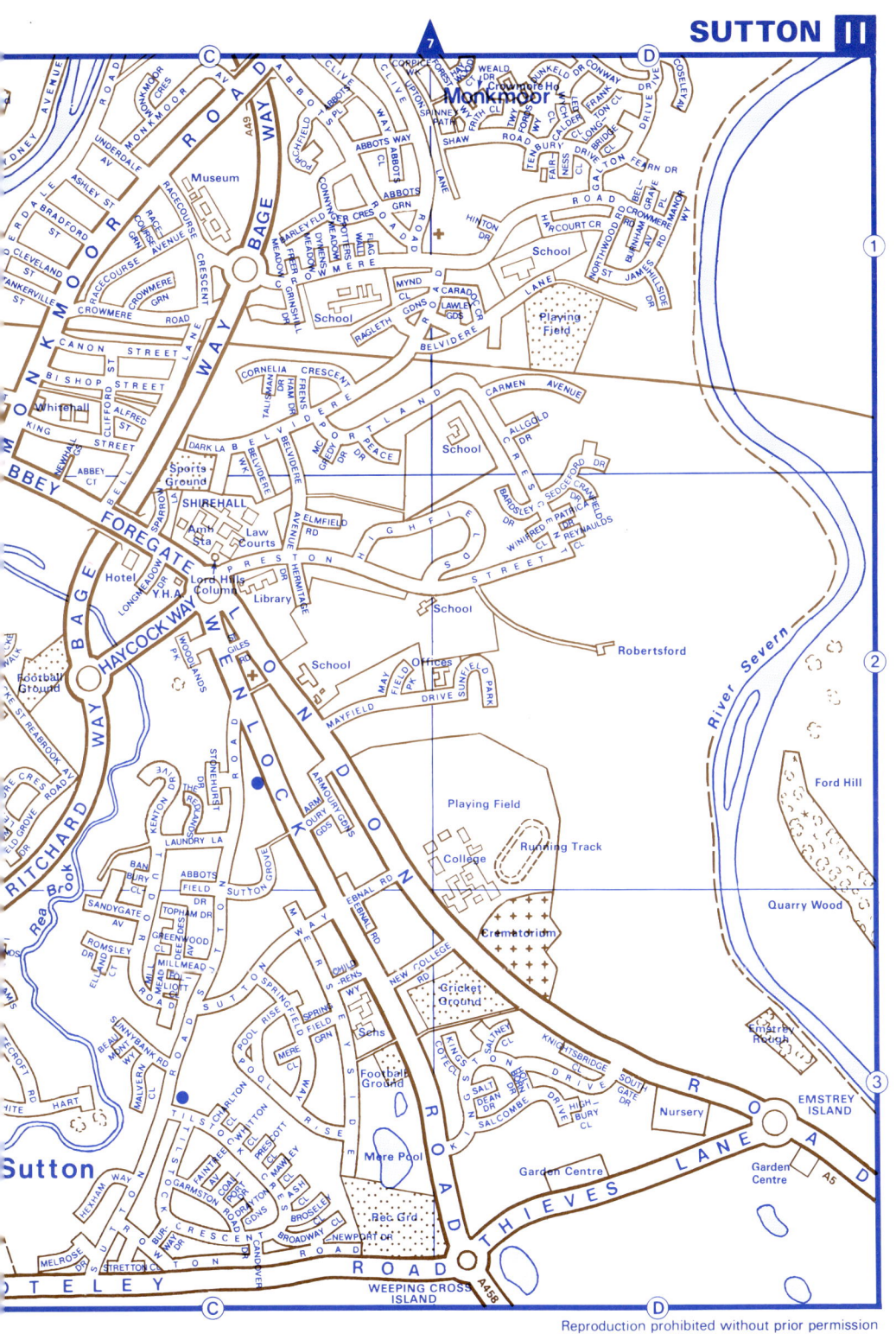

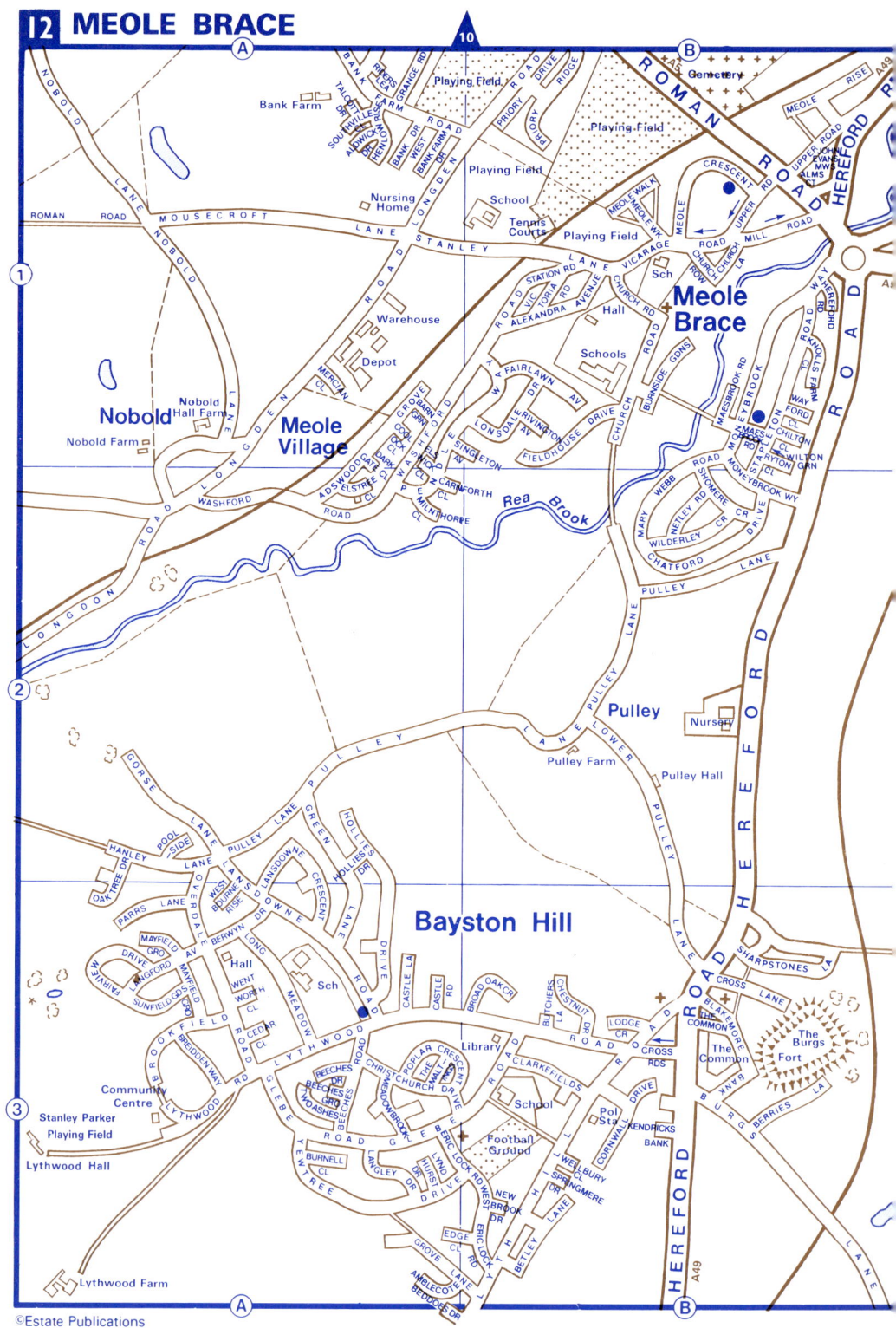

10

A

B

Nobold

Nobold Farm

Nobold Hall Farm

Meole Village

Meole Brace

Bayston Hill

Pulley

Pulley Farm

Pulley Hall

Nursery

Bank Farm

Nursing Home

School

Tennis Courts

Playing Field

Playing Field

Playing Field

Playing Field

Cemetery

Warehouse

Depot

Schools

Hall

Rea Brook

Gorse Lane

Hanley

Pool Side

Parrs Lane

Mayfield Gro

Langford

Hall

Sch

Went Worth Cl

Cedar Cl

Community Centre

Stanley Parker Playing Field

Lythwood Hall

Lythwood Farm

Library

School

Football Ground

The Burgs Fort

The Common

Sharpstones

Cross Lane

Pol Sta

ROMAN ROAD

MOUSECROFT LANE

ROMAN ROAD

WASHFORD ROAD

HEREFORD ROAD

HEREFORD ROAD

PULLEY LANE

LONGDON ROAD

©Estate Publications

1

2

3

A49

A5

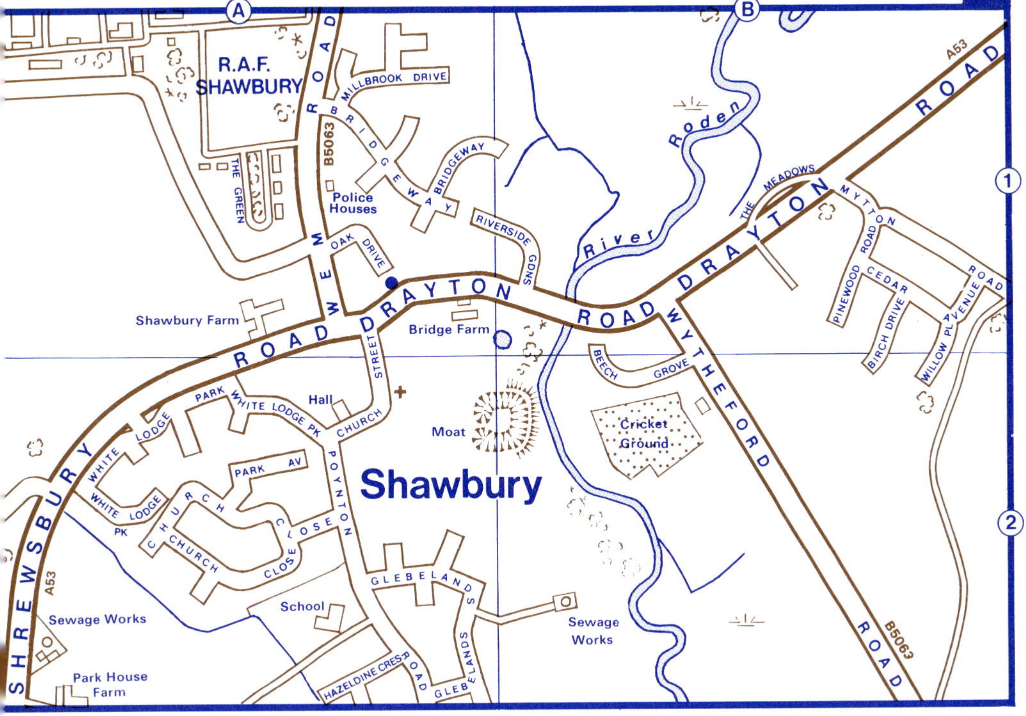

R.A.F. SHAWBURY

A53

ROAD

Roden

The Meadows

MILLBROOK DRIVE

B5063

BRIDGEWAY

BRIDGEWAY

Police Houses

RIVERSIDE GDNS

River

MYTTON ROAD

PINEWOOD ROAD

CEDAR ROAD

BIRCH DRIVE

WILLOW AVENUE

ROAD

OAK DRIVE

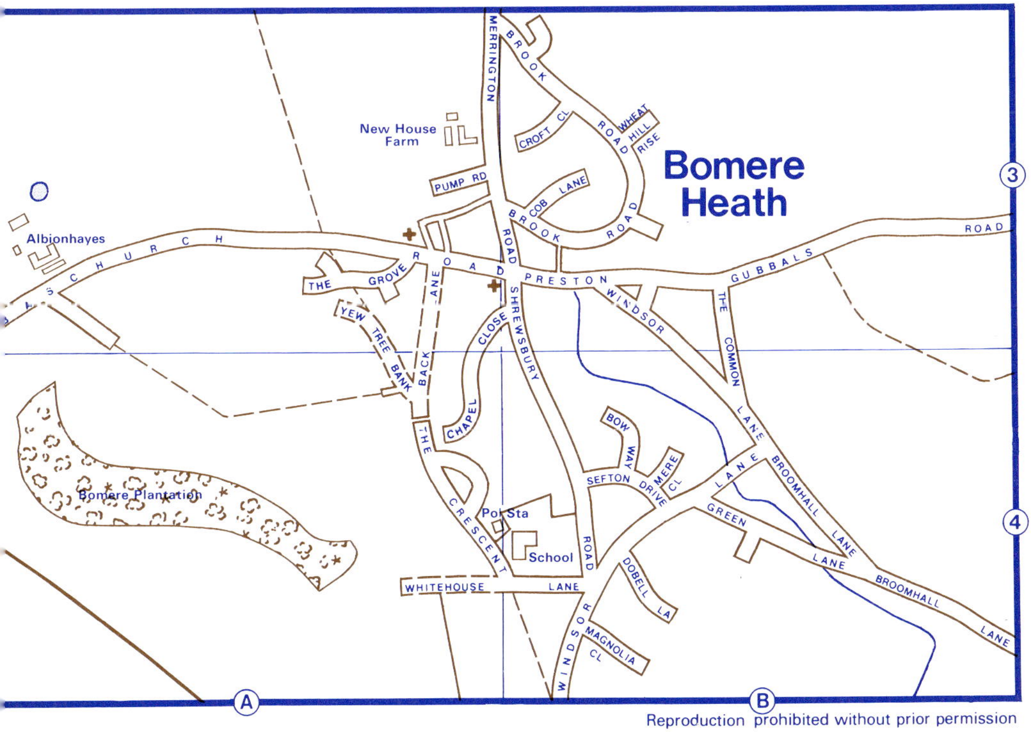

ROAD DRAYTON ROAD

DRAYTON ROAD

WYTHEFORD

Shawbury Farm

STREET

Bridge Farm

BEECH

GROVE

Shawbury Farm

Hall

WHITE LODGE PK

PARK

CHURCH

Moat

Cricket Ground

SHREWSBURY

WHITE LODGE

PARK AV

CLOSE

POYNTON

Shawbury

A53

WHITE LODGE PK

CHURCH

CHURCH CLOSE

ROAD

B5063

Sewage Works

School

GLEBELANDS

GLEBELANDS

Sewage Works

Park House Farm

HAZELDINE CRES

GLEBELANDS ROAD

MERRINGTON

BROOK

New House Farm

CROFT CL

WHEAT HILL

ROAD

RISE

PUMP RD

COB LANE

BROOK

ROAD

Bomere Heath

ROAD

Albionhayes

ST'S CHURCH

THE GROVE

LANE

ROAD

PRESTON

GUBBALS

ROAD

YEW TREE BANK

BACK LANE

SHREWSBURY

WINDSOR

THE COMMON LANE

Bomere Plantation

CLOSE

CHAPEL

BOW WAY

BOMERE CL

BROOMHALL LANE

CRESCENT

SEFTON DRIVE

LANE

GREEN

LANE

Por Sta

School

WHITEHOUSE LANE

ROAD

DOBELL LA

MAGNOLIA CL

WINDSOR ROAD

BROOMHALL LANE

LANE

INDEX TO STREETS

The Index includes some names for which there is insufficient space on the maps. These names are preceded by an * and are followed by the nearest adjoining thoroughfare.

Abbey Ct	11 C1	Beehive La	10 A2	Cartland Av	7 D3	Crawford Meadow	9 D2
Abbey Foregate	5 C2	Belgrave Pl	11 D1	Cartmer Dri	7 C1	Crescent La	5 B2
*Abbeydale, Holywell St	10 B1	Bell La	11 C2	Castle Foregate	5 B1	Cressage Av	6 B2
Abbots Clo	11 C1	Belle Vue Gdns	10 B2	Castle Gates	5 B1	Crewe St	6 B3
Abbots Field Dri	11 C2	Belle Vue Rd	5 C2	Castle La	12 A3	Crocus Dri	10 B2
Abbots Grn	11 C1	Bellstone	5 B2	Castle Rd	12 A3	Croft Clo	13 B3
Abbots Rd	11 C1	Belmont	5 B2	Castle St	5 B1	Cross Hill	5 B2
Abbots Way	11 C1	Belmont Bank	5 B2	Castle Walk	5 C1	Cross Hill Ct	5 B2
Abingdon Rd	7 C3	Belvidere Av	11 C1	Cathrines Dri	9 D2	Cross La	12 B3
Adams Ridge	10 B2	Belvidere La	11 C1	Cedar Av	13 B1	Cross Rds	12 B3
Adswood Gro	12 A2	Belvidere Rd	11 C1	Cedar Clo	12 A3	Crowmeole Dri	9 D2
Ainsdale Dri	7 C2	Belvidere Walk	11 C1	Cedars Dri	6 B2	Crowmeole La	9 D2
Alan Guttridge Dri	9 D2	Benyon St	10 B1	Central Dri	10 A2	Crowmere Grn	11 C1
Alberbury Dri	7 D1	Berries La	12 B3	Chaffinch Way	7 D1	Crowmere Rd	11 C1
Albert Rd	7 C2	Berrington Dri	6 B2	Chapel Clo	13 A3	Curlew Clo	7 D1
Albert Sq	7 C2	Berwick Av	6 A3	Chapel Hill	8 A2		
Albert St	5 C1	Berwick Clo	6 A3	Chapel St	5 A1	Dale Rd	7 C3
Aldwick Dri	12 A1	Berwick Rd	6 A2	Charlton Clo	11 C3	Dark Gate Clo	12 A1
Alexandra Av	12 B1	Berwyn Dri	12 A3	Chatford Dri	12 B2	Dark La	11 C1
Alfred St	11 C1	Betley La	12 B3	Chester St	5 B1	Darville	7 C3
Allerton Rd	7 D2	Betton St	5 C2	Chestnut Dri	12 B3	Darwin Gdns	5 A1
Allestree Clo	6 B1	Bewdley Av	7 D3	Chestnut Gro	9 D1	Darwin St	5 A1
Allgold Dri	11 D1	Bexfield	10 A1	Chevin Clo	6 B1	Deedes Av	11 C3
Allness Clo	7 D3	Bicton La	8 A1	Childrens Way	11 C3	Deepfields	9 D2
Alma Ct	10 A3	Birch Dri	13 B1	Chilton Clo	12 B1	Derfald St	6 B3
Alma St	5 A1	Birchwood Dri	6 B1	Christchurch Dri	12 A3	Derwent Av	6 B1
Alms Ct	10 A3	Bishop St	11 C1	Church Clo, Bicton	8 A1	Dickens Pl	9 D2
Alton Ter	5 C2	Blakemore Bank	12 B3	Church Clo, Shawbury	13 A2	Didcot Clo	7 C3
Amber Hill	9 D2	Blakeway Mews	8 A2	Church La, Bicton	8 A1	Ditherington Rd	7 C2
Amblecote	12 A3	Boscombe Dri	6 B1	Church La, Meole Brace	12 B1	Dobell La	13 B4
Arbourne Gdns	10 B2	Bow Way	13 B4	Church Rd, Meole Brace	12 B1	Dogpole	5 B2
Argyle St	6 B3	Brackwell Dri	9 D2	Church Rd, Shawbury	13 A2	Dorset St	5 C1
Arlington Way	7 D1	Bradford St	11 C1	Church Row	12 B1	Dounton Clo	7 C1
Armdale	7 C3	Bramley Clo	7 C3	Church St	5 B1	Downfield Rd	9 D1
Armoury Gdns	11 C2	Breidden Vw	10 A1	Churchill Rd	9 D2	Downing Clo	9 D2
Ash Clo	11 C3	Breidden Way	12 A3	Claremont Bank	5 A1	Drawell St	10 B3
Ashfields Rd	6 B2	Bridge St	5 A1	Claremont Hill	5 A1	Drayton Gdns	11 C3
Ashford Dri	6 B1	Bridgeford Way	7 C3	Claremont St	5 B1	Drayton Rd	13 A1
Ashley St	11 C1	Bridgeway	13 A1	Clarkefields	12 B3	Drinkwater St	5 A1
Ashton Rd	5 A2	Briery La	8 A2	Claverley Cres	7 D2	Dunbar	6 B1
Aspen Gro	9 D2	Brightwell	10 B3	Claverley Rd	7 D2	Dunedin Dri	9 D2
Aston Butts	7 C3	Brixton Way	7 C1	Cleveland St	11 C1	Dunkeld Dri	11 D1
Avondale Dri	6 B3	Broad Haven Clo	6 B2	Clifford St	11 C1	Dutton Grn	6 B1
Aynesworth Grn	7 C1	Broad Oak Cres	12 B3	Clifton Rd	6 B1	Dymens Meadow	11 C1
Aysgarth Rd	9 D1	Broadway Clo	11 C3	Clive Grn	7 C3		
		Bromfield Dri	11 C2	Clive Rd	11 C1	Earls Hill Vw	8 A3
Back La	13 A4	Bromley Rd	8 A2	Clive Way	11 C1	Earlswood	8 B3
Back Lime St	5 B2	Brook Rd, Bomere Heath	13 B3	Coach Rd	8 A2	East Cres	7 C2
Bage Way	11 C2	Brook Rd, Shrewsbury	5 C2	Coalport Dri	11 C3	Eastwood Rd	9 D1
Bagley Dri	6 B2	Brook St	10 B3	Cob La	13 B3	Ebnal Rd	11 C3
Bakewell Clo	6 B1	Brookfield	12 A3	Cokayne Grn	6 B1	Ebury Av	7 D2
Balliol Way	9 D2	Brookside	8 A1	Coleham	5 C2	Edge Clo	12 B3
Banbury Clo	11 C2	Broomhall La	13 B4	Coleham Head	5 C2	Edgefield Grn	8 A2
Bank Dri West	12 A1	Broseley Clo	11 C3	College Hill	5 B2	Egland La	5 C2
Bank Farm Dri	12 A1	Broughton Rd	7 D2	Colmere Dri	6 B2	Elder Dri	9 D1
Bank Farm Rd	12 A1	Brunel Way	10 B2	Combermere Dri	6 B2	Elland Ct	11 C3
Bardsley Dri	11 D2	Burey St	10 B2	Comet Dri	7 C3	Ellesmere Dri	6 B3
Barker St	5 A1	Burgs La	12 B3	Coniston Rd	7 C2	Ellesmere Rd	6 B2
Barley Field	11 C1	Burnell Clo	12 A3	Conney Grn	8 A2	Elm St	6 B3
Barn Grn	12 PA1	Burnham Av	11 D1	Connynger Cres	11 C1	Elmfield Rd	11 C2
Barn Rd	9 D1	Burnside Gdns	12 B1	Conway Dri	7 C3	Elstree Clo	12 A2
Barracks La	9 D1	Burton St	10 B1	Coolock Clo	12 A1	Elswick Clo	12 A1
Barton Clo	7 C3	Burway Dri	11 C3	Copperfield Dri	9 D2	English Bri	5 C2
Baschurch Rd	13 A3	Butcher Row	5 B1	Coppice Walk	11 C1	Ennerdale Rd	7 C2
Battlefield Rd	7 C1	Butchers La	12 B3	Copthorne Cres	10 A1	Eric Lock Rd	12 B3
Bayford Dri	6 B2	Butler Rd	10 A2	Copthorne Dri	10 A1	Eric Lock Rd West	12 A3
Beacalls La	5 C1	Buttercup Way	10 B2	Copthorne Gdns	9 D1	Eskdale Rd	7 D3
Beachley	7 C2	Butterwick Dri	6 B2	Copthorne Pk	9 D1		
Beaufort Grn	7 C1	Buttington Rd	7 C3	Copthorne Rise	5 A1	Fairburn Dri	9 D2
Beaumont Way	11 C3	Byfield	7 C2	Copthorne Road	5 A1	Fairfield Dri	12 A3
Beddoes Dri	12 B4	Bynner St	10 B2	Cordon Clo	7 C2	Fairford Pl	5 C2
Beech Gro	13 B2			Cordon Cres	7 C2	Fairlawn Av	12 B1
Beeches Dri	12 A3	Cadogan Gdns	10 A1	Cordon Dri	7 C2	Fairness Clo	11 C1
Beeches Gro	12 A3	Calcot La	8 A2	Cordon Rd	7 C2	Falcons Way	9 C2
Beeches La	5 B2	Calder Clo	11 D1	Cornelia Cres	11 C1	Falstaff St	5 A1
Beeches Rd	12 A3	Camross Dri	6 B2	Corner Farm Dri	8 A3	Far Garden Pl	6 B3
Beechwood Dri	6 B2	Candover Dri	11 C3	Corner La	8 A2	Farfield Clo	8 B2
		Canon St	11 C1	Cornwall Dri	12 B3	Farmoor	7 D2
		Canon Vale	10 A2	Corporation La	6 A3	Fearn Dri	11 D1
		Canonbury	5 A2	Corset Clo	6 B1	Featherbed La, Bicton	8 B1
		Caradoc Cres	11 D1	Coseley Av	7 D3	Featherbed La, Harlescott	7 C1
		Cardington Dri	6 B1	Cotes Cres	8 A2	Felcourt Dri	8 B2
		Carlton Clo	9 C1	Coton Cres	6 B3	Felton Clo	6 B3
		Carmen Av	11 D1	Coton Mount	6 A3	Ferndale Rd	7 D2
		Carnforth Clo	12 A2	Cotshore Dri	9 D3	Fernlea Croft	8 A2
		Caroline Cres	5 C2	Cranfield Dri	11 D2	Field Clo	7 C1

Fieldhouse Dri 12 B1
First Av 7 C2
Fish St 5 B1
Fitzalan Rd 7 C1
Flag Wall 11 C1
Folliott Clo 11 C3
Forest Way 11 D1
Fox Glove Clo 10 B2
Foxley Gro 8 A2
Frankton Clo 11 D1
Frankwell 5 A1
Frankwell Quay 5 A1
Freer Meadow 11 C1
Frensham Dri 11 C1
Freshfields 7 C1
Frith Clo 11 D1

Gains Av 8 A2
Gains Park Way 8 A2
Galton Dri 11 D1
Garmston Rd 11 C3
Gasworks La 10 B1
Glamis 11 C3
Glebe Rd 12 A3
Glebelands 13 A2
Glenburn Gdns 7 D3
Glendower Ct 3 B3
Gloucester Rd 6 B1
Goldcrest Dri 7 D2
Gorse La 12 A2
Grange Rd 12 A1
Grangefields Rd 10 A2
Gransden Dri 9 B2
Grantley Av 8 B2
Granville St 10 A1
Grasmere Rd 7 C2
Gravel Hill La 6 A3
Green Clo 13 B4
Green La, Bayston Hill 12 A2
Green La,
    Bomere Heath 13 B4
Green Ways 12 A1
Greenacre Rd 9 D1
Greenfield St 6 B3
Greenhill Av 5 A1
Greenwood Clo 11 C3
Greville Rd 1C A3
Grey Stone Ct 8 A3
Greyfriars Rd 5 C2
Grinshill Dri 11 C1
Grope La 5 B1
Grosvenor Grn 7 C1
Grove La 12 A3
Grove Rd 11 C2

Hafren Clo 5 A1
Hafron Rd 10 A1
Hamilton Dri 7 D3
Hampton Rd 6 B3
Hanley La 12 A2
Hanwood Rd 9 D2
Harcourt Cres 11 D1
Hardwick Dri 9 C1
Harlescott Clo 7 C1
Harlescott Cres 7 C1
Harlescott La 7 C1
Harley Dri 6 B2
Haughmond Av 7 C1
Haughmond Ter 6 B3
Havelock Rd 10 B2
Hawkstone Rd 7 C1
Hawthorn Rd 10 B2
Haycock Way 11 C2
Haywood Ct 11 D1
Hazeldine Cres 13 A2
Hazledine Way 10 B3
Hearne Way 7 C3
Heaton Clo 9 D2
Henlow Rise 12 A1
Hereford Rd 12 B1
Hermitage Dri 11 C2
Hermitage Walk 5 A1
Heron Dri 7 D1
Hexham Way 11 C3
High Oak 8 A2
High Ridge Way 9 D2
High St 5 B1
Highbury Clo 11 D3

Highfields 11 C2
Highgate Dri 10 A3
Hill Cres 10 A2
Hills La 5 B1
Hillside Dri 11 D1
Hinton Dri 11 D1
Hodgkinson Walk 6 B1
Holborn Dri 11 D3
Holgate Dri 7 D2
Hollies Dri 12 A2
Holyhead Rd 8 A1
Holywell St 10 B1
Honeysuckle Row 10 B3
Hopton Dri 7 D2
Hordley Av 6 B1
Horksley 6 B1
Horsefair 5 C1
Hotspur St 6 B3
Howard St 5 C1
Hunter St 5 A1

Isle La 8 A1
Ivy Hatch 7 C2

John Evans Mews 10 A3
John St 6 B3
Judith Butts Gdns 7 C3
Judith Butts La 7 C3

Keble Way 9 D2
Kelsall Dri 8 A2
Kemble Dri 9 D2
Kemps Eye Av 10 B3
Kendal Rd 7 C1
Kendal Rd North 7 C1
Kendricks Bank 12 B3
Kenley Av 6 B2
Kennedy Rd 10 A2
Kenton Dri 11 C2
Kenwood Dri 9 D1
Kenwood Gdns 9 D2
Kenwood Rd 9 D1
Kestrel Dri 7 D1
King St 11 C1
Kingfisher Clo 7 D2
Kings Cote Clo 11 D3
Kingsland Bri 5 A2
Kingsland Bridge App 5 A2
Kingsland Rd 5 B2
Kingston Dri 11 D3
Kingswood Cres 9 C1
Kingswood Rd 9 C1
Kirkland Av 8 B2
Knightsbridge Clo 11 D3
Knolls Farm Clo 12 B1
Knowsley Dri 8 A2
Kynaston Rd 7 C1

Lady Leasows 10 A3
Ladycroft Clo 9 D2
Lancaster Rd 6 B2
Lanesfield 9 D2
Langford Av 12 A3
Langford Grn 7 C1
Langholm Dri 7 D3
Langley Dri 12 A3
Langtree Dri 6 B2
Lansdowne Cres 12 A3
Lansdowne Rd 12 A2
Lapwood Dri 6 B2
Larkhill Rd 9 C1
Laundry La 11 C2
Lavender Way 10 B2
Lawley Gdns 11 D1
Leafields 7 C1
Leamore Cres 11 C2
Ledwych Clo 11 D1
Leeswood Ct 8 A3
Leighton Rd 6 B2
Lesley Owen Way 7 C2
Lessar Av 5 A1
Leven Dri 7 C2
Leyburn Av 9 D1
Lime St 5 B2
Lindale Ct 10 A1
Linden Gdns 10 B2
Lindley St 10 B1
Lingen Clo 7 C3

Links Rd 10 B3
Linnet Clo 7 D1
Little Harlescott La 6 B1
Little Over Av 6 B1
Lockwood Dri 6 B2
Lodge Cres 12 B3
London Rd 11 C2
Long Meadow 12 A3
Long Pack 7 D1
Long Row 6 B2
Longbridge Clo 11 D1
Longden 5 B2
Longden Av 10 B2
Longden Gdns 5 B2
Longden Grn 10 A2
Longden Gro 10 B2
Longden Rd 12 A1
Longmeadow Dri 11 C2
Longner St 5 A1
Longville Rd 6 B1
Lonsdale Dri 12 B1
Loton Butts 7 C3
Lovat Clo 7 D3
Lower Claremont Bank 5 A1
Lower Pulley La 12 B2
Lowfield 7 C3
Lox Dale 9 D3
Luciefelde Rd 10 B2
Ludford Dri 6 B2
Lydham Rd 6 B1
Lymehurst Ct 6 B3
Lyndhurst Dri 12 A3
Lyth Hill Rd 12 B3
Lythwood Rd 12 A3

McGredy Dri 11 C1
Maesbrook Rd 12 B1
Magnolia Clo 13 B4
Mallard Clo 7 D1
Malvern Clo 11 C3
Manor Way 11 D1
Maple Dri 6 B2
Mardol 5 B1
Mardol Gdns 5 B1
Mardol Head 5 B2
Marine Ter 5 C2
Market St 5 B1
Marl Pool Clo 9 D2
Marton Dri 6 B2
Mary Webb Rd 12 B2
Massey Cres 6 B1
Mawley Clo 11 C3
Mayfield Dri 11 C2
Mayfield Gro 12 A3
Mayfield Pk 11 C2
Meadow Clo 7 D2
Meadow Farm Dri 7 C1
Meadow Pl 5 B1
Meadowbrook 12 A3
Melbourne Rise 8 A2
Melrose Dri 11 C3
Melton Way 9 D3
Meole Crescent 12 B2
Meole Rise 12 B1
Meole Walk 12 B1
Mercian Clo 12 A1
Mere Clo,
    Bomere Heath 13 B4
Mere Clo, Sutton 11 C3
Meregreen Ct 9 D3
Merlin Rd 9 C1
Merrington Rd 13 A3
Merseyside 11 C3
Middlegate 6 B1
Middletown Sq 7 D3
Milk St 5 B2
Mill Rd 12 B1
Millbrook Dri 13 A1
Millers Grn 7 C3
Millmead 11 C3
Milnthorpe Clo 12 A2
Milton Clo 7 C3
Mitcham Ct 8 B2
Moneybrook Way 12 B1
Monkmoor Av 11 C1
Monkmoor Cres 11 C1
Monkmoor Rd 11 C1
Montague Pl 10 B2

Montrose Pl 8 A3
Moreton Cres 5 C2
Mornington Clo 9 D1
Morris Walk 6 B1
Mortimar 7 C1
Morville Rd 6 B2
Moss Bank Way 9 D1
Moston Grn 7 D2
Moston Rd 7 D2
Motters Head 6 B1
Mount Pleasant Rd 6 B1
Mount St 5 A1
Mousecroft La 12 A1
Murivance 5 A2
Mynd Clo 11 C1
Mytton Gro 9 D1
Mytton Oak Rd 9 C2
Mytton Pk 9 D1
Mytton Rd 13 B1

Nealors La 10 A1
Nether Way 9 D2
Netley Rd 12 B2
Nettles La 5 A1
New Brook Dri 12 B3
New College Rd 11 C3
New Field Dri 6 B3
New Park Clo 6 B3
New Park Rd 6 B3
New Park St 10 B1
New St 5 A1
Newent Clo 7 C3
Newhall Gdns 11 C1
Newport Dri 11 C3
Nightingale Walk 6 B1
Nobold La 12 A1
North Clo 10 A2
North Hermitage 10 B2
North St 10 B1
Northside Clo 7 D2
Northumberland Pl 6 B3
Northwood Rd 11 D1

Oak Dri 13 A1
Oak La 9 C1
Oak St 10 B3
Oakdale Dri 9 D2
Oakfield Dri 9 D2
Oakfield Rd 9 D1
Oakhurst Dri 6 B2
Oakley Av 10 B2
Oakley St 10 B2
Oaktree Dri 12 A2
Oakwood Dri 6 B2
Old Coleham 5 C2
Old Heath 7 C2
Old Roman Rd 10 A2
Onslow Dri 6 B2
Oriel Way 9 D2
Orsons Meadow 8 A2
Oteley Rd 10 B3
Outwood 6 B1
Overcross 10 B3
Overdale Rd 12 A2
Overstone 6 B1
Overton Clo 7 D2

Painswick Clo 8 A2
Paintree Av 11 C3
Park Av, Shawbury 13 A2
Park Av, Shrewsbury 5 A1
Parrs La 12 A3
Partridge Clo 7 D1
Patricia Dri 11 D2
Peace Dri 11 C1
Pembroke Way 9 D2
Pendle Way 12 A2
Pengrove 5 B2
Pengwern Clo 10 A1
Pengwern Rd 10 A1
Pensfold 8 A3
Percy St 6 B3
Percy St North 6 B3
Perivale Clo 9 D2
Pig Trough 6 B3
Pinewood Clo 6 B2
Pinewood Rd 13 B1
Pitchford Rd 6 B1
Pool Rise 11 C3

Poolside 12 A2
Poplar Cres 12 A3
Porchfield 11 C1
Porthill Dri 10 A1
Porthill Gdns 10 A1
Porthill Rd 10 A1
Portland Cres 11 C1
Potters Meadow 11 C1
Pound Clo 5 C2
Powis Dri 6 B2
Poynton Dri 6 B2
Poynton Rd 13 A2
Prescott Clo 11 C3
Prestbury Grn 7 C1
Preston Gubbals Rd 13 B3
Preston St 11 C2
Pride Hill 5 B1
Primrose Dri 10 B3
Princess St 5 B2
Priory Dri 12 B1
Priory Ridge 12 B1
Priory Road 5 A1
Pritchard Way 11 C2
Pulley La 12 B2
Pulrose Walk 10 B3
Pump La 9 C1
Pump Rd 13 A3

Quarry Av 5 A1
Quarry Pl 5 A2
Quatford Clo 7 D2
Queen St 10 B1

Raby Cres 10 B2
Racecourse Av 11 C1
Racecourse Cres 11 C1
Racecourse Grn 11 C1
Racecourse La 9 C1
Rad Valley Gdns 9 D2
Rad Valley Rd 9 D2
Radbrook Rd 9 D2
Ragleth Gdns 11 C1
Raven Meadows 5 B1
Ravenscourt Walk 9 C2
Rea St 10 B2
Reabrook Av 11 C2
Red Barn La 10 A2
Redfern Clo 10 B3
Regents Dri 7 C3
Reynaulds Clo 11 D2
Richmond Dri 9 D1
Ridgebourne Rd 9 D2
Riverdale Rd 7 C3
Rivers Lea 12 A1
Riverside 5 B1
Riverside Gdns 13 B1
Rivington Av 12 B1
Robin Clo 7 D1
Rocke St 11 C2
Rocke Walk 11 C2
Roman Rd,
  Meole Brace 12 B1
Roman Rd, Nobold 12 A1
Romsley Dri 11 C3
Rosedale 7 C2
Roselyn Field Cres 7 C2
Rosemede 7 C2
Roseway 7 C2
Rotherfield 7 C2
Rothley Clo 9 D2
Rothley Dri 8 A2
Roundhill Grn 6 A3
Roundhill La 6 A3
Roundway 10 B3
Roushill 5 B1
Roushill Bank 5 B1
Rowton Rd 11 C3
Russell Field 9 D2
Russell Ridge 9 D2
Rutland 7 C1
Rydal Av 7 C2
Ryelands 9 D2
Ryton Clo 12 B1

St Almkond Sq 5 B1
St Andrews Rd 9 D2
St Annes Rd 9 D2
St Antonys Rd 9 D2
St Austin Friars 5 A1

St Austins St 5 A1
St Chads Ter 5 A2
St Georges St 5 A1
St Giles Rd 11 C1
St James Rd 11 D1
St Johns Hill 5 A2
St Julians Friars 5 B2
St Marys Ct 5 B2
St Marys Pl 5 B1
St Marys St 5 B1
St Marys Water La 5 B1
St Michaels St 6 B3
St Michaels Ter 6 B3
Salamanca Av 9 D1
Salcombe Dri 11 D3
Salendine 6 B2
Saltdean St 11 D3
Salters La 5 C2
Saltney Clo 11 D3
Sandford Av 6 B2
Sandford Clo 6 B2
Sandiway 9 D2
Sandleigh 8 B2
Sandygate Av 11 C3
Sapcote La 8 A2
Sawston Clo 9 D2
Saxon Ct 8 B3
School Gdns 5 B1
School La 5 C2
Scott St 10 B2
Seabury Clo 10 B2
Sedgeford Dri 11 D2
Sefton Dri 13 B4
Selwyn Clo 9 D2
Severn Bank 5 C1
Severn St 10 B1
Sharpstones La 12 B3
Shaw Rd 11 D1
Shelton Circle 9 C1
Shelton Cres 9 C1
Shelton Fields 9 D1
Shelton Gdns 9 C1
Shelton La 9 D1
Shelton Pk 9 D1
Shelton Rd 9 D1
Shepherds La 8 A2
Sherbourne Rd 9 D1
Shomere Cres 12 B2
Shop Latch 5 B2
Shorncliffe Dri 9 D1
Shorncliffe Way 9 D1
Shrewsbury Rd,
  Bomere Heath 13 B3
Shrewsbury Rd,
  Shawbury 13 A2
Silverdale 8 A3
Silverstone Clo 8 B3
Simpsons Sq 6 B3
Singleton Av 12 A1
Sion Dri 8 A2
Six Acres 9 D3
Smithfield Rd 5 B1
Snowdrop Clo 10 B3
South Clo 10 A2
South Hermitage 10 B2
Southgate Dri 11 D3
Southville Clo 12 A1
Spa St 10 B2
Sparkham Clo 9 D2
Sparrow La 11 C2
Spinney Path 11 D1
Spring Gdns 6 B3
Springfield Grn 11 C3
Springfield Way 11 C3
Springmere Dri 12 B3
Squires Ct 8 A2
Squirrel Walk 8 A2
Stanhill Rd 9 D3
Stanley La 12 A1
Stanton Grn 7 D2
Stapleton Rd 12 B1
Station Rd 12 B1
Steepside 9 D2
Stephenson Dri 10 B2
Stilton Clo 9 D2
Stokesay Av 6 B2
Stonehurst Dri 11 C2
Stretton Clo 11 C3
Strickland 6 B1

Sultan Rd 6 B3
Summit Clo 10 B3
Sundorne Av 7 C2
Sundorne Clo 7 C2
Sundorne Cres 7 C2
Sundorne Rd 7 C2
Sunfield Gdns 12 A3
Sunfield Pk 11 D2
Sunnybank Rd 11 C3
Sussex Dri 10 B3
Sutton Gro 11 C3
Sutton La 10 B3
Sutton La, Belle Vue 10 B2
Sutton Rd 11 C3
Sutton Way 11 C3
Swallow Dri 7 D1
Swan Hill 5 B2
Swift Clo 7 D1
Swiss Farm Rd 9 D1
Sydney Av 7 C3
Syersacre Rd 6 B1

Talcott Dri 12 A1
Talisman Dri 11 C1
Tankerville St 11 C1
Tansley Clo 9 D2
Tarvin Rd 6 B3
Tawnylea 6 B2
Telford Way 7 C2
Tenbury Dri 11 D1
The Bell 8 A3
The Birches 13 A3
The Bradleys 7 D1
The Broad Wall 9 D3
The Cinder Path 10 A3
The Common,
  Bomere Heath 13 B3
The Common,
  Meole Brace 12 B3
The Crescent 13 A4
The Dana 5 C1
The Green 13 A1
The Grove 13 A3
The Hassacks 7 D2
The Hawthorns 10 B2
The Hig 7 D1
The Keep 8 A2
The Knolls 8 A2
The Lees 8 A2
The Mall 5 B1
The Maltings 12 A3
The Meadows 13 B1
The Mount 9 D1
The Oaklands 8 A2
The Orchard 8 A2
The Oval 8 A1
The Paddocks 8 A3
The Parade 5 B1
The Parks 7 D1
The Redlands 11 C2
The Ridings 8 A3
The Rocks 10 B3
The Springs 7 D1
The Square 5 B2
The Woolams 8 A2
The Yeld 8 A3
Thieves La 11 D3
Thomas Ct 5 C2
Thornhill Rd 9 D1
Thorns Gro 8 A2
Tilbrook Dri 7 C3
Tilstock Cres 11 C3
Topham Dri 11 C3
Torrin Dri 9 D2
Town Walls 5 B2
Tresta Clo 10 A3
Trinity St 10 B2
Tudor Rd 11 C2
Two Ashes 12 A3
Twyfords Way 11 D1

Underdale Av 11 C1
Underdale Rd 11 C1
Uplands Dri 11 C3
Upper Rd 12 B1
Uppington Av 10 B2
Upton La 11 C1

Vane Rd 10 A2

Vennington Walk 7 C3
Vicarage Rd 12 B1
Victoria Av 5 A2
Victoria Rd 12 B1
Victoria St 5 C1
Victoria Ter 10 B1
Victorian Arcade 5 B1

Waincott 6 B1
Walkford Clo 9 D2
Walnut Dri 6 B1
Walton Rd 10 B3
Warrenby Clo 7 C3
Washford Rd 12 A2
Water St 10 B1
Waverton Way 8 B2
Wayford Clo 12 B1
Wayhill 6 B1
Weald Dri 11 D1
Wellbury Clo 12 B3
Wellmeadow Dri 9 D1
Wellmeadow Gdns 9 D1
Wellmeadow Rd 9 D1
Wellwood Clo 9 C1
Welsh Bri 5 A1
Welshpool Rd 9 C1
Wem Rd 13 A1
Wendsley Rd 6 B1
Wenlock Rd 11 C2
Wentworth Clo 12 A3
West Edge 8 A3
West Hermitage 10 B2
West St 10 B1
Westbourne Rise 12 A3
Westbury Rd 6 B1
Westhope Av 9 C1
Westlands Rd 9 D1
Weston Dri 6 B2
Westmoreland Mews 6 B3
Westwood Dri 9 D1
Wheathill Rise 13 B3
Whiston Clo 9 D2
Whitchurch Rd 7 C2
White Bank 8 A2
White Hart 10 B3
White House Gdns 6 B3
White Lodge Pk 13 A2
Whitecote Dri 8 A2
Whitecroft Rd 10 B3
Whitehall St 10 B1
Whitehouse La 13 A4
Whitemere Rd 6 B2
Whittington Clo 7 D2
Whitton Clo 11 C3
Wilderley Cres 12 B2
Wildon Way 9 D2
Willington Clo 6 B1
Willow Pl, Copthorne 9 D1
Willow Pl, Shawbury 13 B1
Wilton Green 12 B1
Windermere Rd 7 C2
Windsor La 13 B3
Windsor Pl 5 B1
Wingfield Clo 6 B3
Wingfield Gdns 6 B3
Winifred Clo 11 D2
Wood St 6 B3
Wood St Gdns 6 B3
Woodcote Way 7 C3
Woodcrest 8 A3
Woodfield Av 9 D1
Woodfield Rd 10 A1
Woodhall Clo 6 B3
Woodlands Pk 11 C2
Woodlark Clo 7 D2
Woodpecker Clo 7 D1
Woodside 8 A1
Woodside Dri 9 D2
Worcester Rd 6 B1
Worrow Dri 8 A2
Worthington Dri 9 D2
Wren Ct 7 D1
Wyebourne Rd 10 A2
Wyle Cop 5 B2
Wytheford Rd 13 B1

Yew Tree Bank 13 A3
Yewtree Dri 12 A3
York Rd 11 C3